MEGAHITS *of* 2011

S0-AUZ-091

11 Pop, Rock, Country, and Movie Chartbusters

ARRANGED BY CAROL MATZ

Contents

Baba Yetu . . . . from *Civilization IV* 2

Forget You . . . . Cee-Lo 10

Honey Bee . . . . Blake Shelton 15

I Love You This Big . . . . Scotty McCreery 20

If I Die Young . . . . The Band Perry 25

Jar of Hearts . . . . Christina Perri 30

Last Friday Night (T.G.I.F.) . . . . . . Katy Perry 38

Lily's Theme . . . . from *Harry Potter and
the Deathly Hallows, Part 2* 35

Statues . . . . from *Harry Potter and
the Deathly Hallows, Part 2* 42

The Story . . . . Brandi Carlile 47

You Might Think . . . . from *Cars 2* 50

Produced by
Alfred Music Publishing Co., Inc.
P.O. Box 10003
Van Nuys, CA 91410-0003
alfred.com

Printed in USA.

ISBN-10: 0-7390-8719-3
ISBN-13: 978-0-7390-8719-0

 Alfred Cares. Contents printed on 100% recycled paper.

Baba Yetu

Music by Christopher Tin
Swahili adaptation of "The Lord's Prayer" by Chris Kiagiri
Arranged by Carol Matz

3

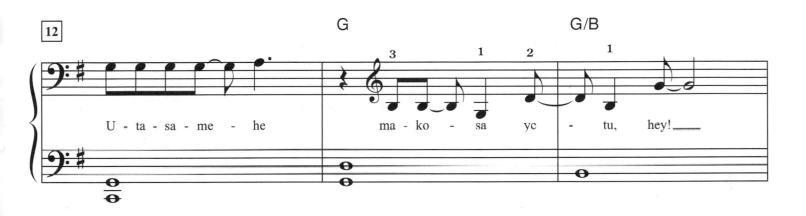

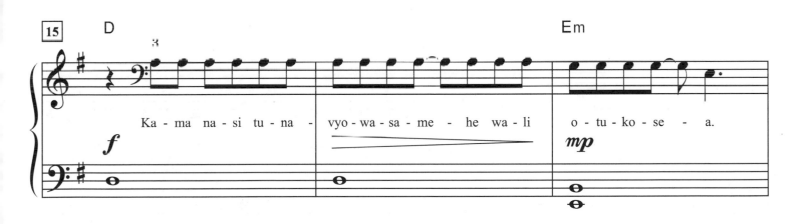

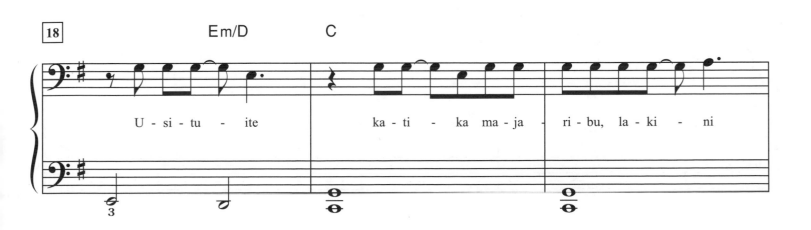

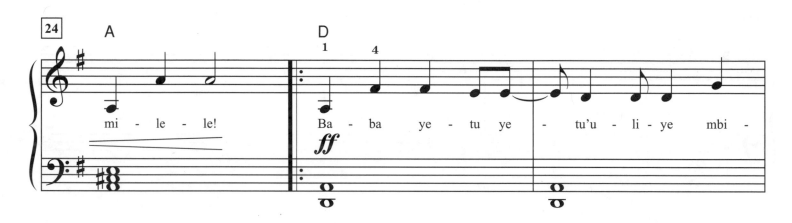

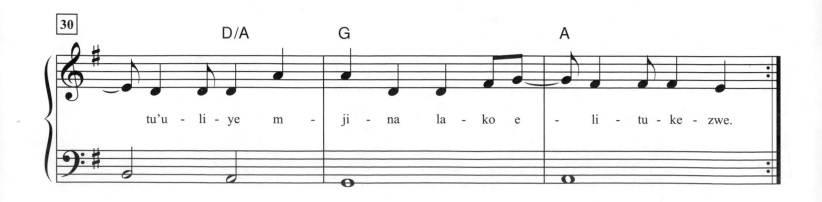

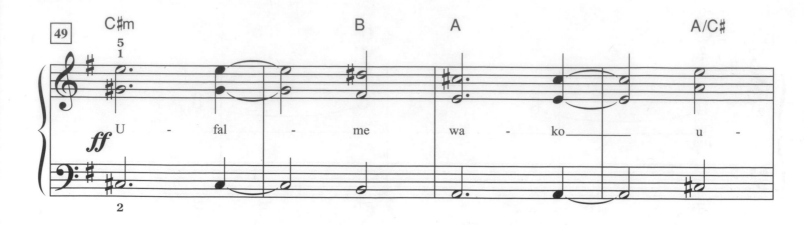

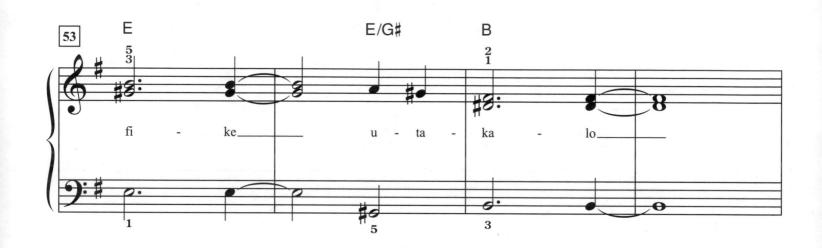

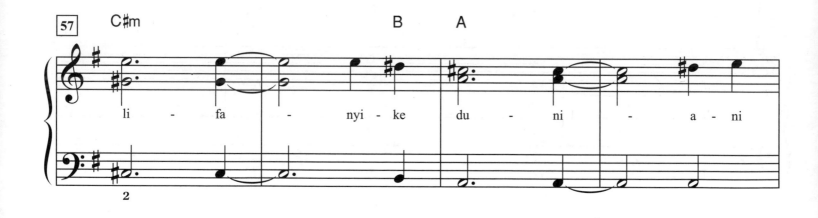

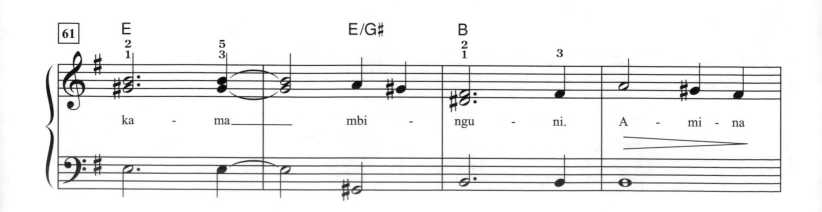

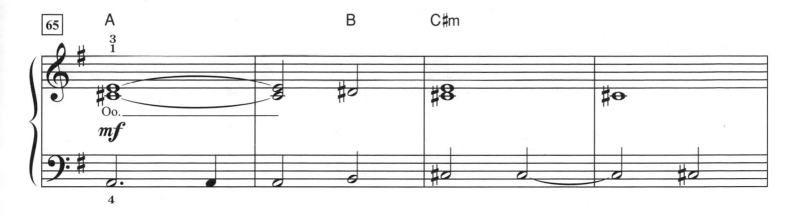

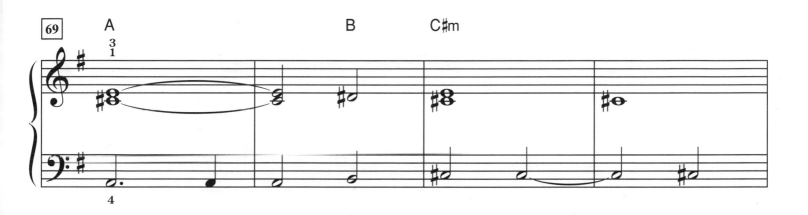

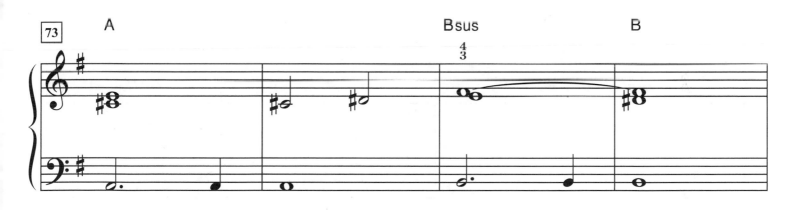

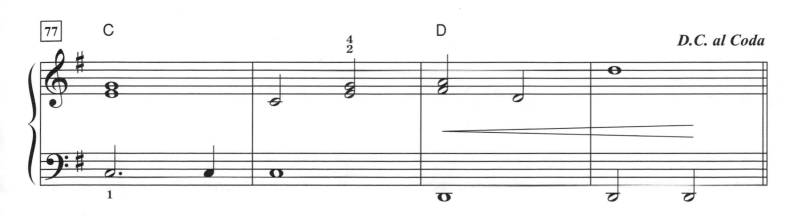

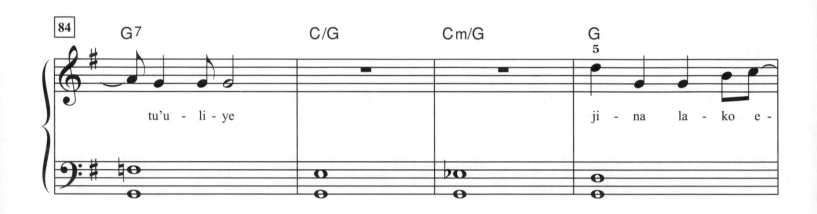

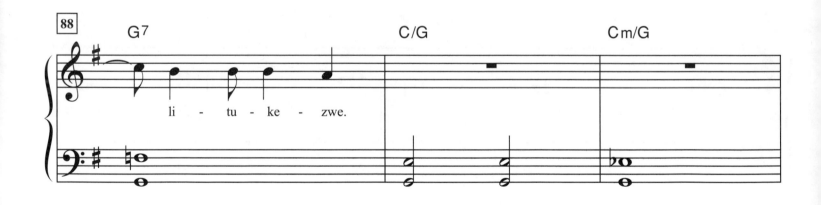

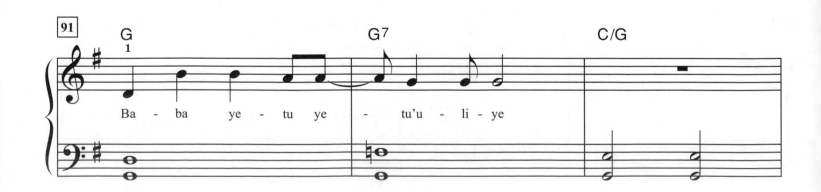

Pronunciation Guide

Ba-ba ye-tu'u-li-ye mbi-ngu-ni ye-tu ye-tu a-mi-na
(Bah-bah yeh-too'oo-lee-yeh mbee-ngoo-nee yeh-too yeh-too ah-mee-nah)

Ba-ba ye-tu-ye-tu'u-li-ye m-ji-na la-ko d-li-tu-ku-zwe
(Bah-bah yeh-too yeh-too'oo-lee yeh ehm-jee-nah-lah-koh eh-lee-too-koo-zweh)

U-tu-pe le-o cha-ku-la che-tu tu-na-cho-hi-ta-ji
(Oo-too-peh leh-oh chah-koo-lah cheh-too too-nah-cho-hee-tah-jee)

U-tu-sa-me-he ma-ko-sa ye-tu
(Oo-too-sah-meh-heh mah-koh-sha yee-too)

Ka-ma na-si tu-na-vyo-wa-sa-me-he wa-li-o-tu-ko-se-a
(Kah-mah nah see too-nah-vyoh-wah-sah-meh-heh wah-lee-oh-too-koh-seh-ah)

U-si-tu-ti-e ka-ti-ka ma-ja-ri-bu
(Oo-see-too-tee-eh kah-tee-kah mah-jah-ree-boo)

la-ki-ni u-tu-o-ko-e na yu-le mu-oo-vu e-mii-le-le
(lah-kee-nee oo-too-oh-koh-eh nah yoo-leh moo-oh-voo eh-mee-leh-leh)

U-fal-me wa-ko u-fi-ke u-ta-ka-lo
(Oh-fahl-meh wah-koh oo-fee-keh oo-tah-kah-loh)

li-fa-nyi-ke du-ni-a-ni ka-ma mbi-ngu-ni
(lee-fah-nyee-keh doo-nee-ah-nee kah-man mbee-ngoo-nee)

Forget You

Words and Music by
Christopher Brown, Peter Hernandez, Ari Levine,
Philip Lawrence and Thomas "Cee Lo" Callaway
Arranged by Carol Matz

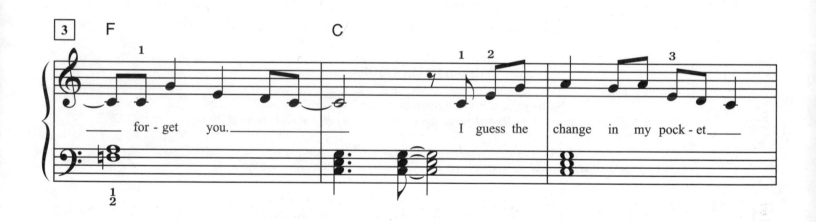

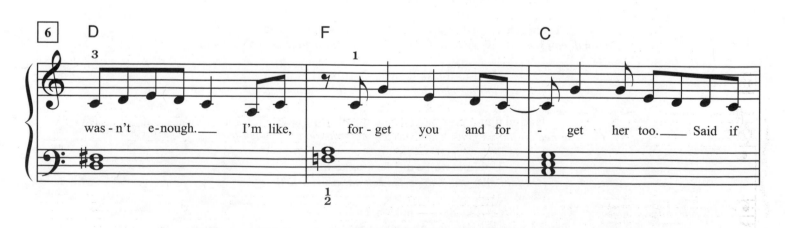

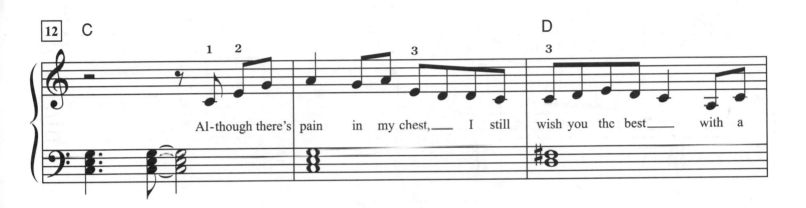

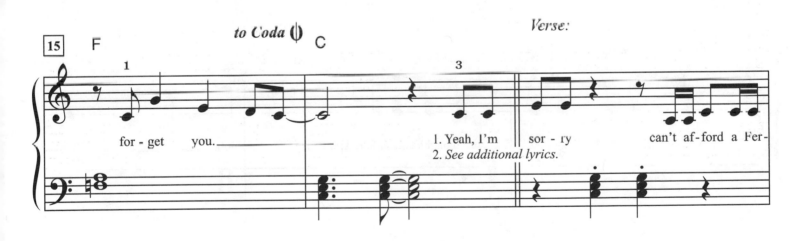

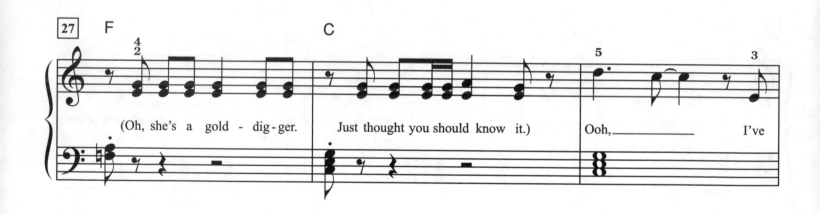

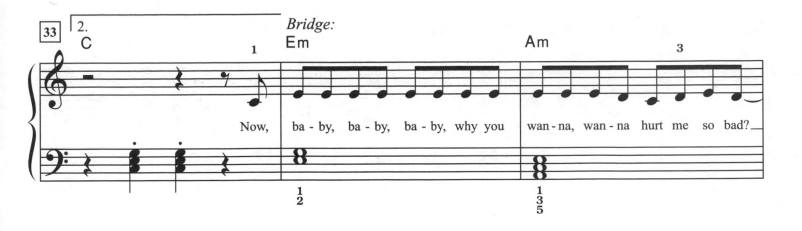

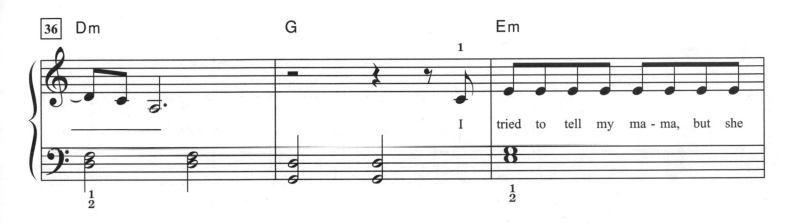

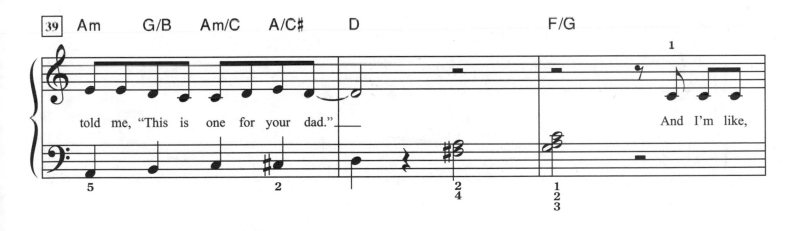

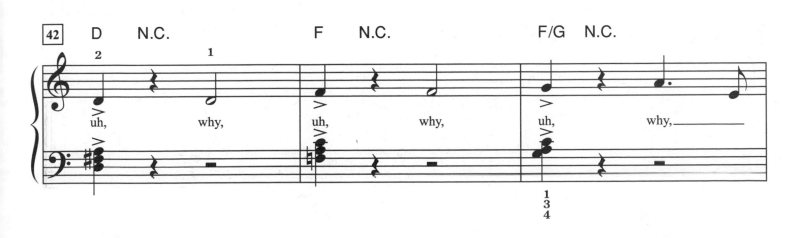

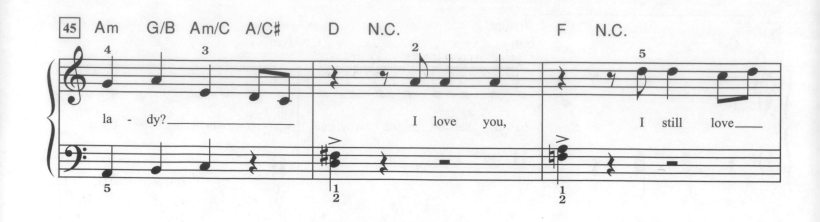

Verse 2:
Now, I know that I had to borrow,
Beg and steal and lie and cheat,
Tryin' to keep ya, tryin' to please ya,
'Cause being in love with your a** ain't cheap.

Honey Bee

Words and Music by
Ben Hayslip and Rhett Akins
Arranged by Carol Matz

Chorus:

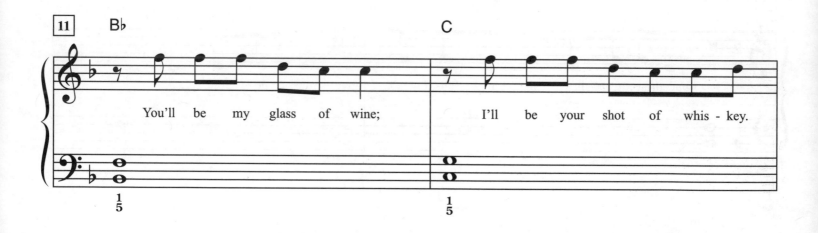

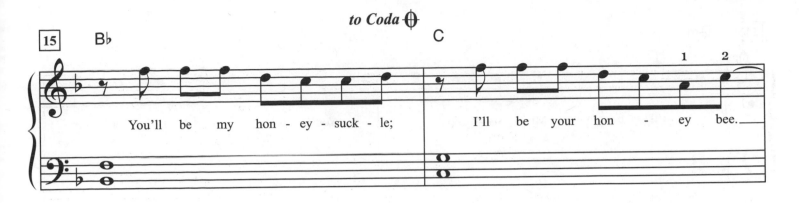

You'll be my hon - ey - suck - le; I'll be your hon - ey bee.

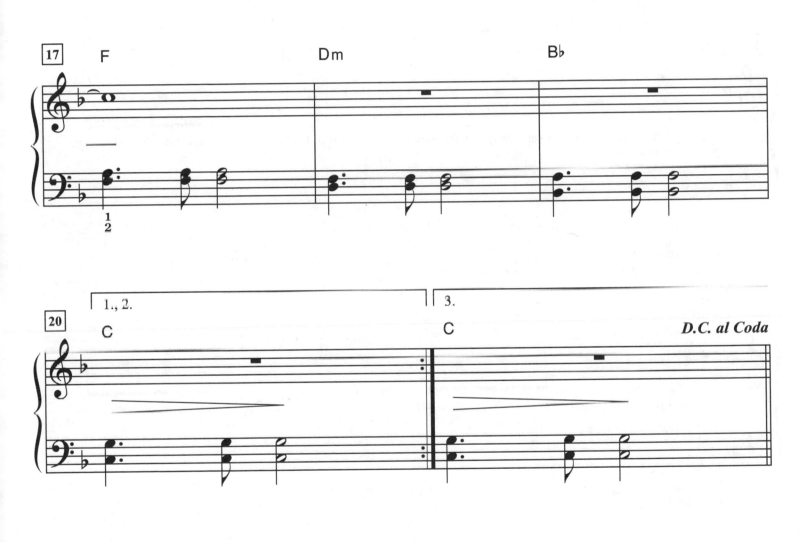

I'll be your hon - ey bee. You'll be my Lou - 'si - an - a;

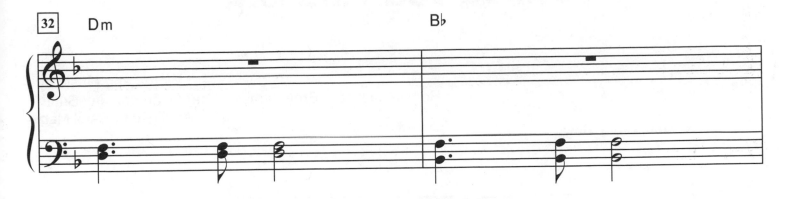

Verse 2:
Yeah, that came out a little country,
But every word was right on the money,
And I got you smilin', honey, right back at me.
Now hold on, 'cause I ain't done;
There's more where that came from.
Well, you know I'm just havin' fun, but seriously.

Chorus 2:
If you'll be my Louisiana, I'll be your Mississippi.
You'll be my little Loretta; I'll be your Conway Twitty.
You'll be my sugar baby; I'll be your sweet iced tea.
You'll be my honeysuckle; I'll be your honey bee.

Verse 3:
Your kiss just said it all.
I'm glad we had this talk.
Nothin' left to do but fall in each other's arms.
I coulda said a "I love you."
I coulda wrote you a line or two.
Baby, all I know to do is speak right from the heart.

I Love You This Big

Words and Music by
Ronnie Jackson, Brett James, Ester Dean and Jay Smith
Arranged by Carol Matz

Moderately slow

Verse:

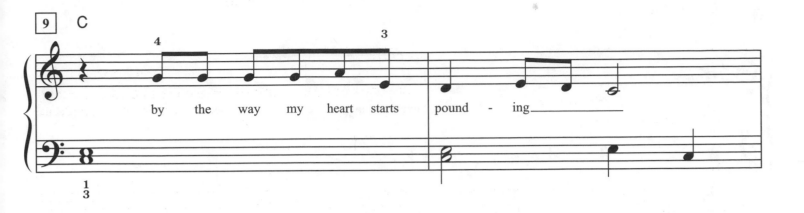

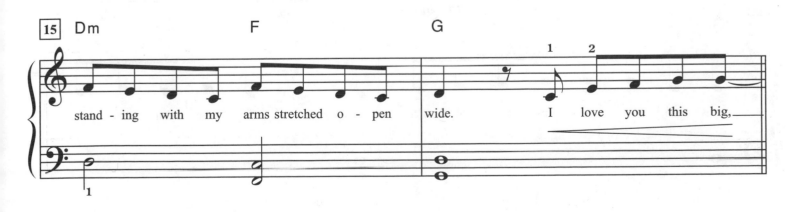

22

17 𝄋 *Chorus:*
C

eyes have nev - er seen. This big,____

19 Am

no one's ev - er dreamed this big.____

21 F

And I'll spend the rest of my life____ ex - plaining what

to Coda ⊕ | 1.

23 G

words can - not de - scribe,____ but I'll try. I love you this____

23

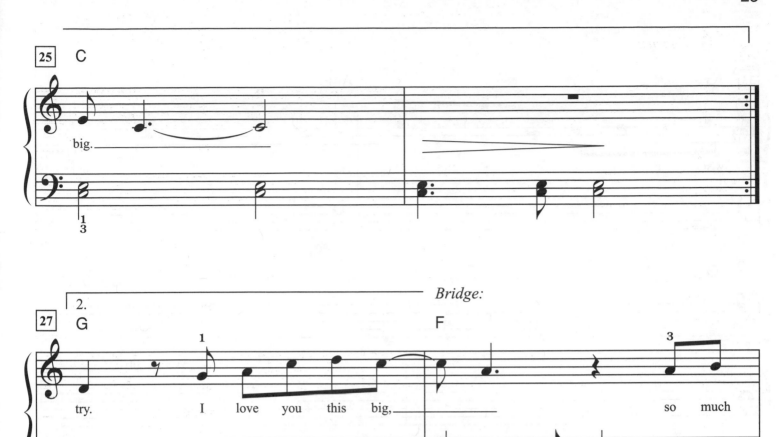

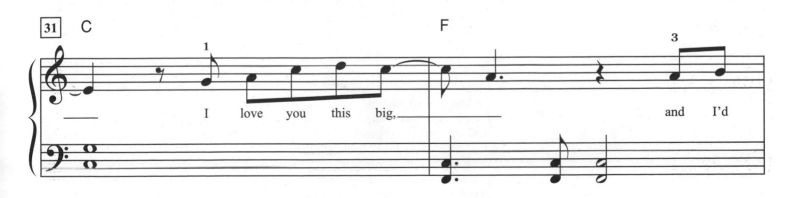

Verse 2:
I'll love you to the moon and back.
I'll love you all the time.
Deeper than the ocean
And higher than the pines.
'Cause girl, you do something to me
Deep down in my heart.
I know I look a little crazy
Standing with my arms stretched all apart.
(To Chorus:)

If I Die Young

Words and Music by Kimberley Perry
Arranged by Carol Matz

26

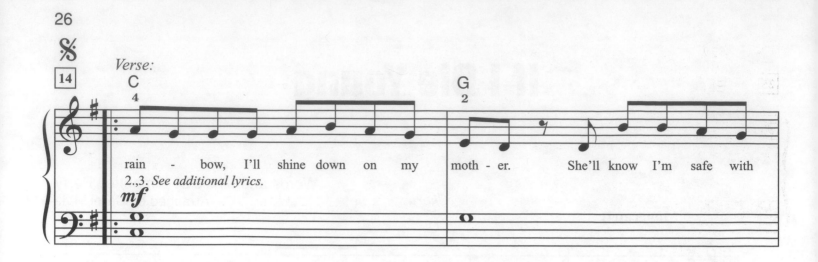

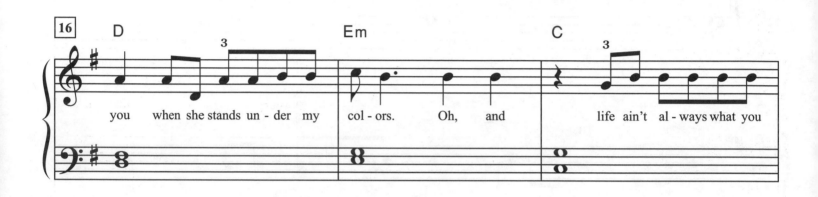

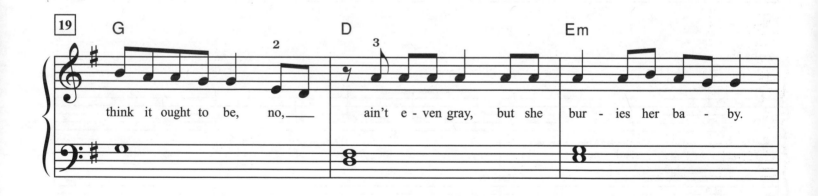

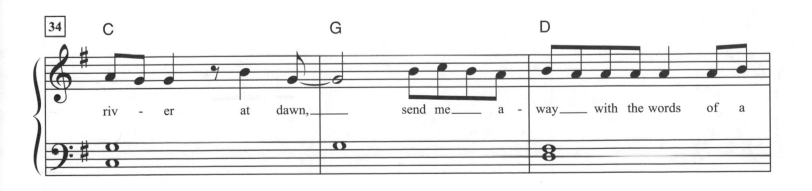

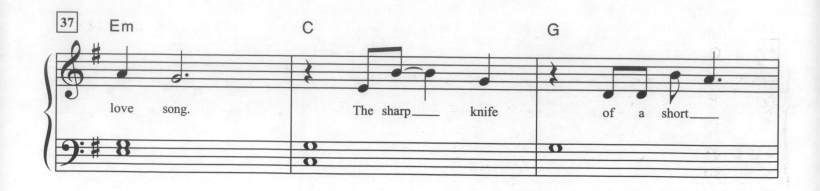

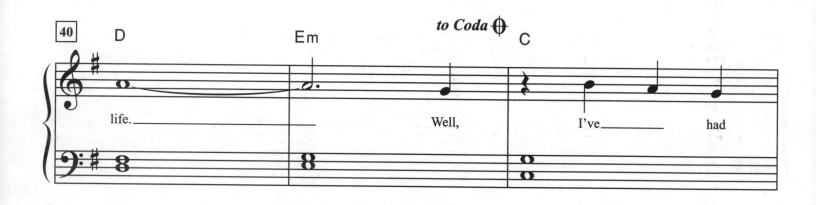

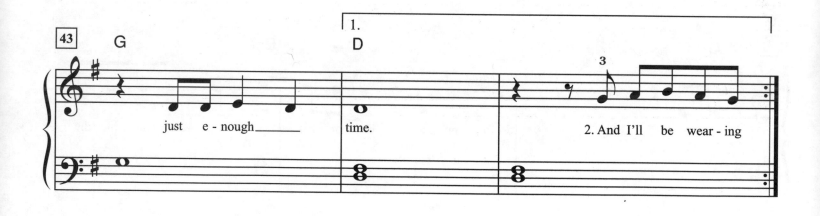

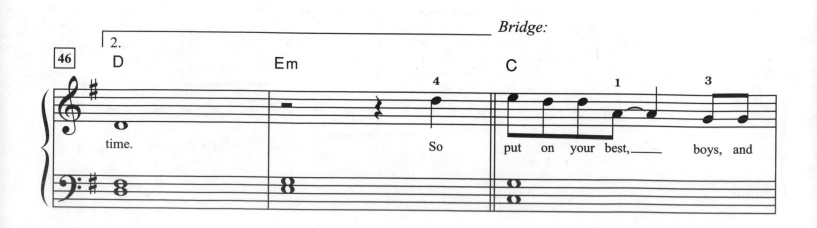

D.S. al Coda

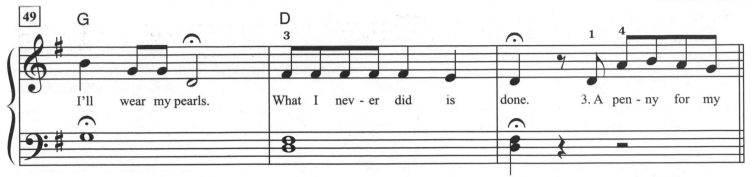

Verse 2:
And I'll be wearing white when I come into your kingdom.
I'm as green as the ring on my little cold finger.
I've never known the loving of a man,
But it sure felt nice when he was holding my hand.
There's a boy here in town, says he'll love me forever.
Who would have thought forever could be severed
By the sharp knife of a short life.
Well, I've had just enough time.

Verse 3:
A penny for my thoughts, oh no, I'll sell them for a dollar.
They're worth so much more after I'm a goner.
And maybe then you'll hear the words I've been singing.
Funny, when you're dead how people start list'nin'.

Jar of Hearts

Words and Music by
Drew Lawrence, Christina Perri and Barrett Yeretsian
Arranged by Carol Matz

31

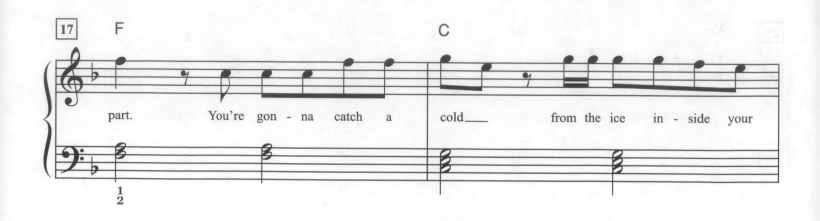

17 F ... C

part. You're gon - na catch a cold___ from the ice in - side your

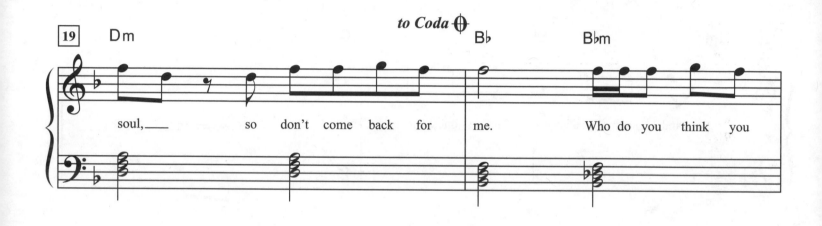

19 Dm ... *to Coda* ⊕ B♭ ... B♭m

soul,___ so don't come back for me. Who do you think you

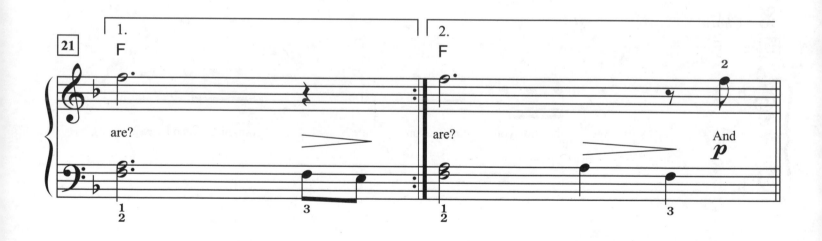

21 1. F ... 2. F

are? ... are? And *p*

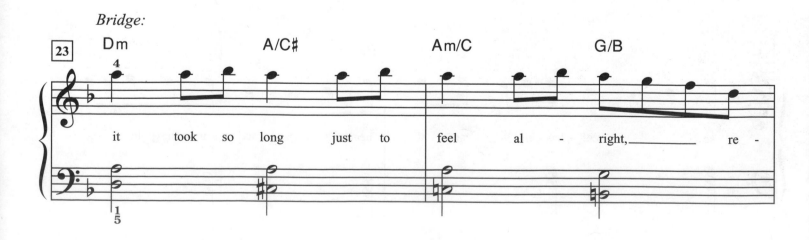

Bridge:

23 Dm ... A/C♯ ... Am/C ... G/B

it took so long just to feel al - right,___ re-

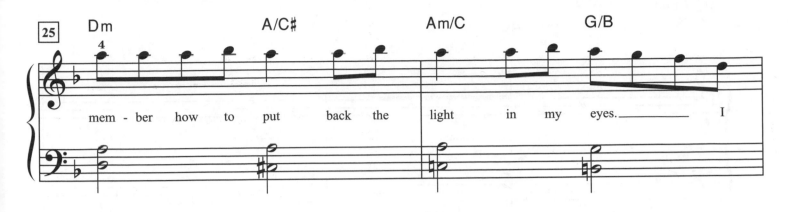

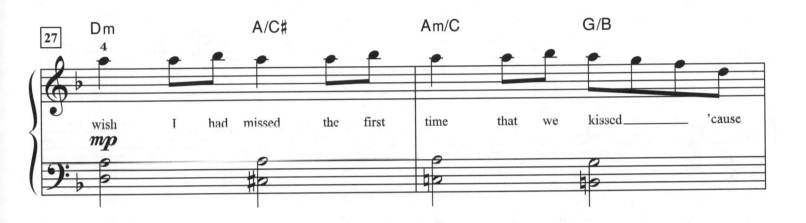

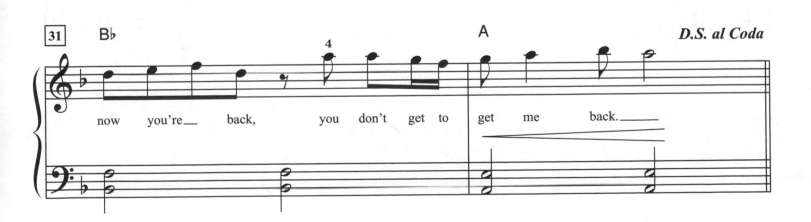

Verse 2:
I heard you're asking all around
If I am anywhere to be found.
But I have grown too strong
To ever fall back in your arms.
And I learned to live half alive,
And now you want me one more time.
(To Chorus:)

Lily's Theme

By Alexandre Desplat
Arranged by Carol Matz

Last Friday Night (T.G.I.F.)

Words and Music by
Katy Perry, Lukasz Gottwald, Max Martin,
Benjamin Levin and Bonnie McKee
Arranged by Carol Matz

Moderately

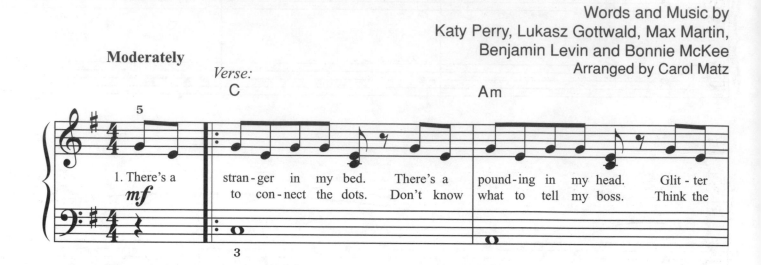

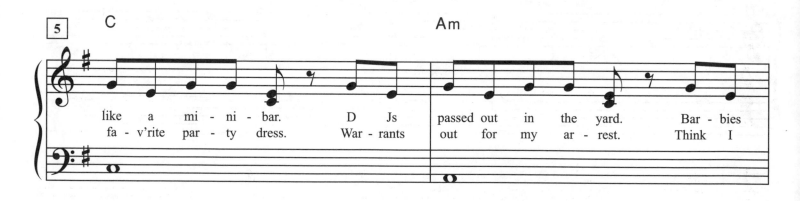

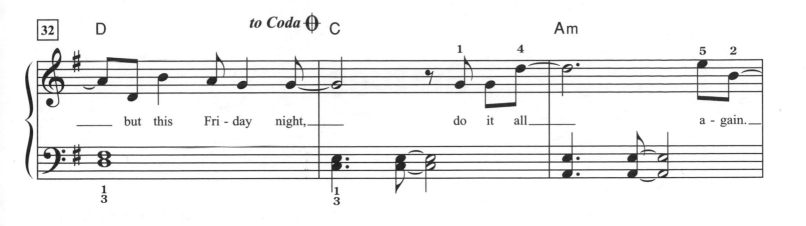

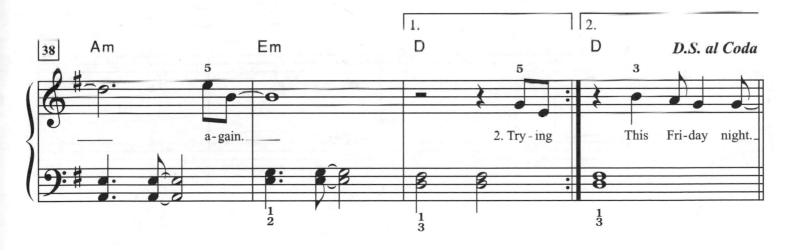

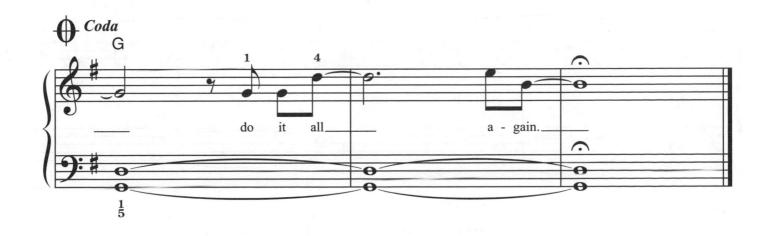

Statues

By Alexandre Desplat
Arranged by Carol Matz

Moderately, with movement

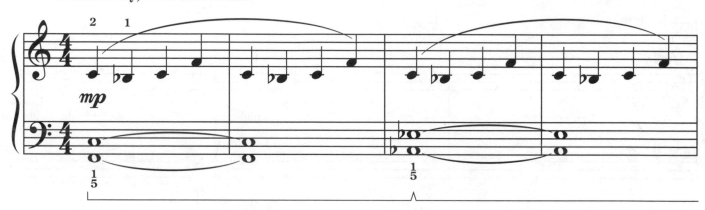

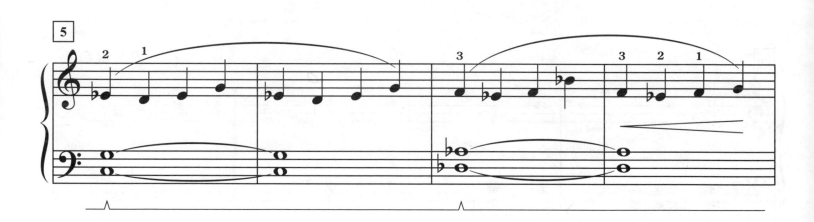

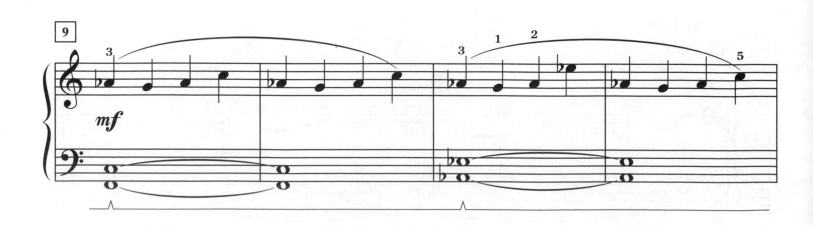

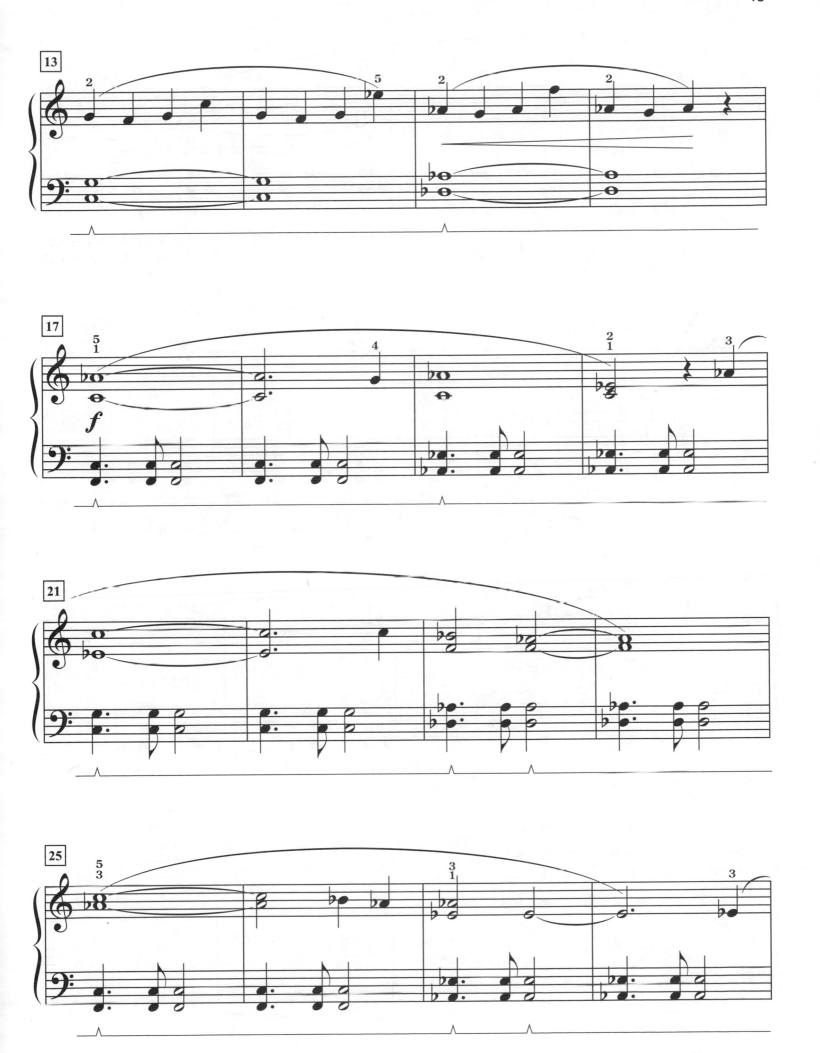

44

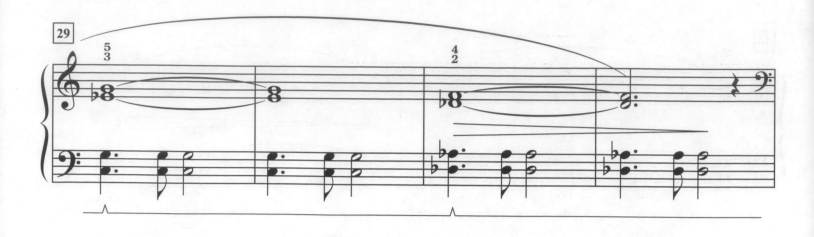

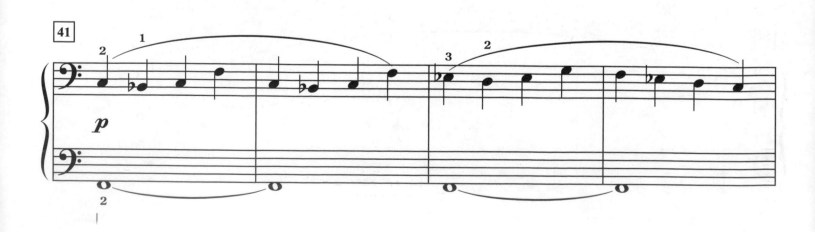

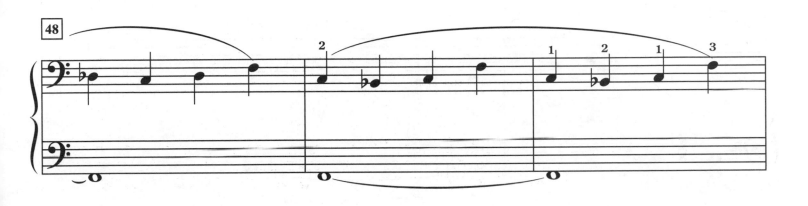

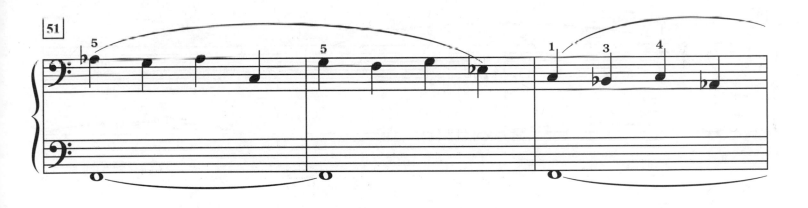

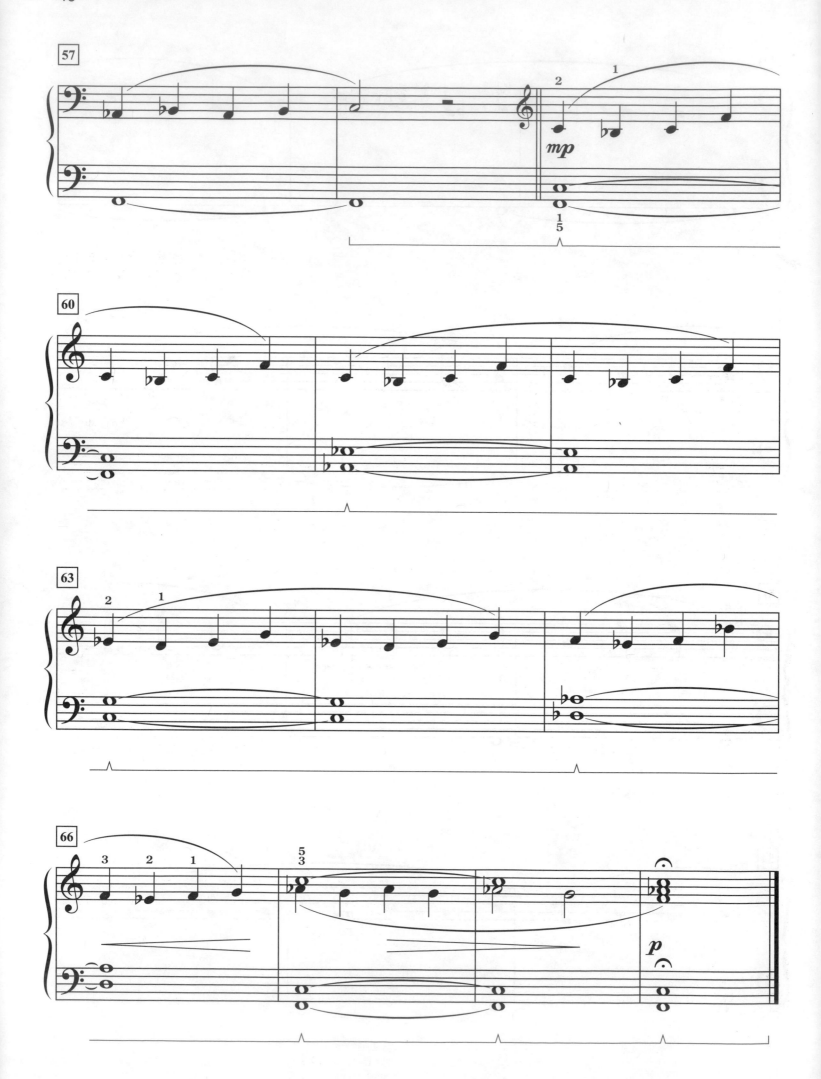

The Story

Words and Music by Phil Hanseroth
Arranged by Carol Matz

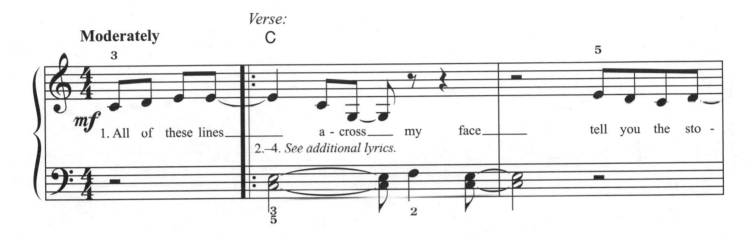

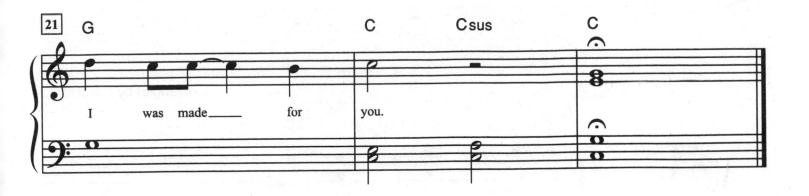

21 G · · · · · C Csus C

I was made_____ for you.

Verse 2:
I climbed across the mountain tops,
Swam all across the ocean blue.
I crossed all the lines, and I broke all the rules,
But, baby, I broke them all for you.
Oh, because even when I was flat broke,
You made me feel like a million bucks. You do.
I was made for you.

Verse 3:
You see the smile that's on my mouth?
It's hiding the words that don't come out.
All of my friends who think that I'm blessed,
They don't know my head is a mess.
No, they don't know who I really am.
And they don't know what I've been through like you do.
And I was made for you.

Verse 4:
All of these lines across my face
Tell you the story of who I am.
So many stories of where I've been
And how I got to where I am.
Oh, but these stories don't mean anything
When you've got no one to tell them to. It's true.
I was made for you.

You Might Think

Words and Music by Ric Ocasek
Arranged by Carol Matz

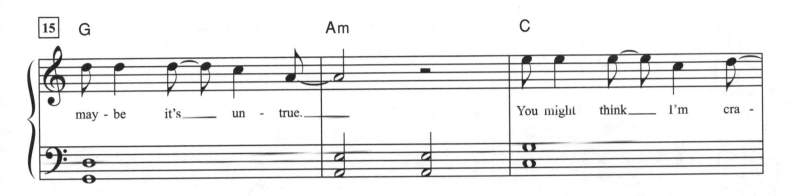

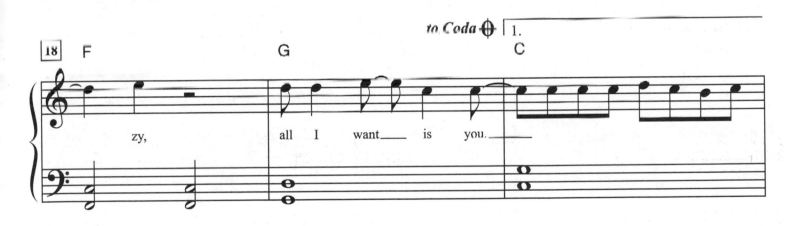

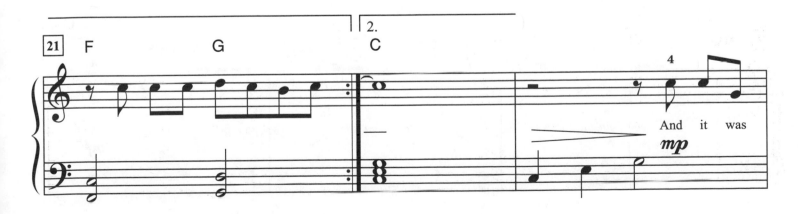

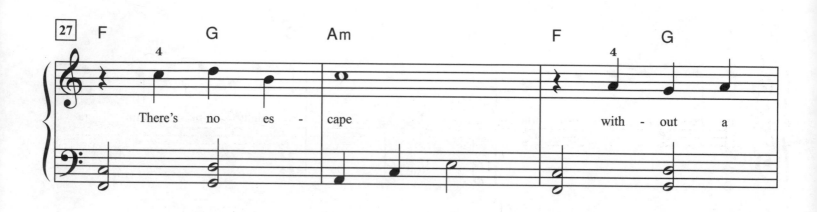

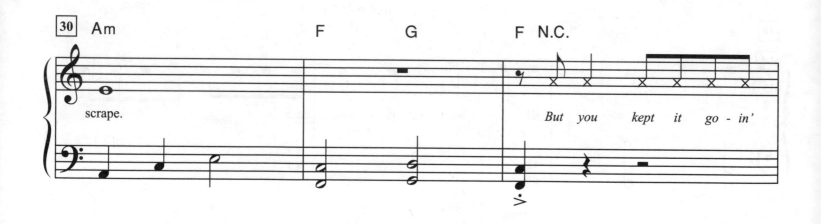

D.S. al Coda

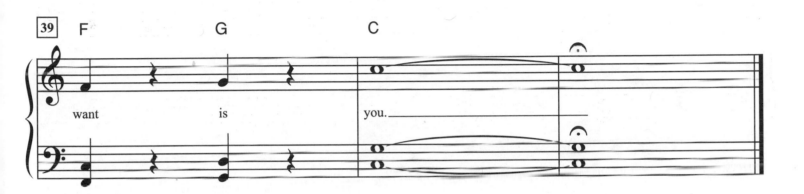

Verse 2:
You might think it's hysterical,
But I know when you're weak.
You think you're in the movies,
And everything's so deep.
But I think that you're wild,
When you flash that fragile smile.
You might think it's foolish,
What you put me through.
You might think I'm crazy,
But all I want is you.

Verse 3:
Well, you might think I'm delirious,
The way I run you down.
But somewhere, sometimes, when you're curious,
I'll be back around.
Oh, I think that you're wild,
And so uniquely styled.
You might think it's foolish,
This chancy rendezvous.
You might think I'm crazy,
But all I want is you.